FREE DVD

Essential Test Tips DVD from Trivium Test Prep

Dear Customer,

Thank you for purchasing from Cirrus Test Prep! Whether you're looking to join the military, get into college, or advance your career, we're honored to be a part of your journey.

To show our appreciation (and to help you relieve a little of that test-prep stress), we're offering a **FREE *NYSTCE Essential Test Tips DVD**** by Cirrus Test Prep. Our DVD includes 35 test preparation strategies that will help keep you calm and collected before and during your big exam. All we ask is that you email us your feedback and describe your experience with our product. Amazing, awful, or just so-so: we want to hear what you have to say!

To receive your **FREE *NYSTCE Essential Test Tips DVD***, please email us at 5star@cirrustestprep.com. Include "Free 5 Star" in the subject line and the following information in your email:

1. The title of the product you purchased.
2. Your rating from 1 – 5 (with 5 being the best).
3. Your feedback about the product, including how our materials helped you meet your goals and ways in which we can improve our products.
4. Your full name and shipping address so we can send your **FREE *NYSTCE Essential Test Tips DVD***.

If you have any questions or concerns please feel free to contact us directly at 5star@cirrustestprep.com. Thank you, and good luck with your studies!

* Please note that the free DVD is <u>not included</u> with this book. To receive the free DVD, please follow the instructions above.

NYSTCE English Language Arts CST (003) Flash Cards Book

RAPID REVIEW TEST PREP INCLUDING MORE THAN 325 FLASH CARDS FOR THE NYSTCE 003 EXAMINATION

Table of Contents

Introduction

Congratulations on choosing to take the New York State Teacher Certification Examinations: English Language Arts Content Specialty Test (003)! By purchasing this book, you've taken the first step toward becoming an English language arts teacher.

This guide will provide you with a detailed overview of the New York State Teacher Certification Examinations: English Language Arts Content Specialty Test (NYSTCE: ELA CST), so you know exactly what to expect on test day. We'll take you through all the concepts covered on the test and give you the opportunity to test your knowledge with practice questions. Even if it's been a while since you last took a major test, don't worry; we'll make sure you're more than ready!

WHAT IS THE NYSTCE?

New York State Teacher Certification Examinations (NYSTCE) are part of a testing program that assesses an examinee's knowledge and skills in accordance with professionally accepted standards of teaching in New York State. The NYSTCE website, www.nystce.nesinc.com, contains information detailing the role of the NYSTCE tests in determining teaching certification and what scores are required.

WHAT'S ON THE ELA CST?

The content in this guide will prepare you for the New York State Teacher Certification Examinations: English Language Arts Content Specialty Test (003). This test assesses whether you possess the knowledge and skills necessary to become a secondary school English language arts teacher using both a multiple-choice section and a written section that includes one constructed-response essay question. This essay question will ask you to evaluate the central idea of a literary work.

You have a maximum of three hours and fifteen minutes to complete the entire test. The test always has a total of ninety multiple-choice questions and one constructed-response question; however, the number of questions specific to each subject is approximate (see the table below). The test makers recommend allotting 135 minutes to the multiple-choice questions and one hour to the constructed response question. Expect to write about 400 – 600 words for the constructed-response question.

What's on the NYSTCE: ELA CST?

Domain	Approximate Number of Questions	Approximate Percentage of Test Score
Reading Literature	15	13%
Reading Informational Texts	15	13%
Writing Arguments	10	9%
Writing Informative and Explanatory Texts	10	9%
Writing Narratives	10	9%
Researching to Build and Present Knowledge	10	9%
Speaking and Listening	10	9%
Language	10	9%
Pedagogical Content Knowledge	1 (constructed response)	20%
Total	**90 multiple choice; 1 constructed response**	**100%**

You will answer approximately fifteen questions (13 percent of the test) about reading literature. This section will require knowledge of major works and authors from around the world, as well as historical movements in literature and the impacts of culture and society on literary movements. Questions will explore literary genres and their major forms, literary elements, poetic devices, and their contributions to a text.

You will answer approximately fifteen questions (13 percent of the test) about reading informational texts. Proficiently reading literary non-fiction is essential to this section. Questions will focus on meaning, overall summation, and effectiveness of texts. Be sure you are aware of the best ways to cull textual evidence from a text to analyze its ideas.

You will answer approximately ten questions (9 percent of the test) about writing arguments. In all of the writing sections, the elements of effective composition, such as eloquent thesis, clear exposition, and concision will be assessed. You will need to understand how writers develop a written argument through textual evidence, diction, structure, appeals, and other rhetorical strategies.

You will answer approximately ten questions (9 percent of the test) about writing informative and explanatory texts. The purpose of explanatory writing is to engage a topic and provide information, so be on the lookout for how different organizational approaches and use of evidence support that purpose.

You will answer approximately ten questions (9 percent of the test) about writing narratives. Narrative writing, used to relate a personal experience, like many types of writing relies on authorial decisions about effective diction and appropriate style and tone.

You will answer approximately ten questions (9 percent of the test) about researching to build and present knowledge. In this section, questions focus on research techniques that expand knowledge and present findings. Know the various aspects of the research process, from selecting a research question to finding credible sources and properly citing them. This section assesses effectively using sources in a text while maintaining flow, originality, and academic integrity.

You will answer approximately ten questions (9 percent of the test) about speaking and listening. In addition to reading and writing skills, as a teacher you will need to communicate with students of different backgrounds and perspectives. Know the purposes and characteristics of effective listening and communication strategies and the barriers that hinder interpersonal exchange. Questions will explore the societal conventions and nonverbal cues that influence communication. Knowledge of diverse learners and the ability to apply pedagogy to reach learners of different needs is essential for this section. Understand how the study of language arts affects your students and can be applied to other aspects of their lives and schoolwork.

You will answer approximately ten questions (9 percent of the test) about language. Generally, this section assesses your ability to follow the conventions of standard American English, including grammar, mechanics, and syntax. Questions in this section will assess your own language and vocabulary usage, as well as your understanding of teaching strategies that reinforce vocabulary and language development. Be aware of how context changes the function of language and may require new perspectives and teaching strategies.

In the constructed-response question, a short textual sample is provided with pertinent discussion points to help you understand the pedagogical importance of the sample and determine how it could best be used in the classroom. You should be able to evaluate student understanding and design instruction that will achieve specific learning goals. Your constructed response must demonstrate your knowledge of pedagogy and application of pedagogical skills.

How is the ELA CST Scored?

On the ELA CST, the number of correctly answered questions is used to create your scaled score. Scores are scaled to a number in the range of 400 – 600; a passing score is 520. The score shows your performance on the test as a whole and is scaled to allow comparison across various versions of the tests. The multiple-choice questions are equally weighted. The 130 multiple-choice questions consist of 80 percent of your overall score, while the constructed-response essay comprises the other 20 percent. There is no guess penalty on the ELA CST, so be sure to eliminate answer choices and answer every question. If you still do not know the answer, guess; you may get it right!

Upon completing your test, you will immediately receive your score. Your score report will be available three to five weeks after testing. Score reports contain the overall scaled score and diagnostic information that indicates your performance on the domains of the test. You can use diagnostic information to better understand your strengths and weaknesses in the material. Scores are automatically added to your certification application file and reported to the New York State Education Department.

HOW IS THE NYSTCE: ELA CST ADMINISTERED?

The NYSTCE English Language Arts Content Specialty Test is available at testing centers across the nation. To find a testing center near you, go to www.nystce.nesinc.com. This is a computer administered test; the website allows you to take tutorials to acclimate yourself to the computerized format.

On the day of your test, be sure to arrive at least thirty minutes early and bring proof of registration and a valid photo ID. You are allowed no personal effects in the testing area and will be provided with a locker to store them. Tobacco products, weapons, and visitors (including friends, relatives, and children) are not permitted in the testing center at all, and bringing those items may be cause for dismissal, forfeiture of your testing fees, and cancellation of your scores. For details on what to expect at your testing center, refer to the NYSTCE website.

ABOUT CIRRUS TEST PREP

Cirrus Test Prep study guides are designed by current and former educators and are tailored to meet your needs as an incoming educator. Our guides offer all of the resources necessary to help you pass teacher certification tests across the nation.

Cirrus clouds are graceful, wispy clouds characterized by their high altitude. Just like cirrus clouds, Cirrus Test Prep's goal is to help educators "aim high" when it comes to obtaining their teacher certification and entering the classroom.

ABOUT THIS GUIDE

This guide will help you master the most important test topics and also develop critical test-taking skills. We have built features into our books to prepare you for your tests and increase your score. Along with a detailed summary of the test's format, content, and scoring, we offer an in-depth overview of the content knowledge required to pass the test. Our sidebars provide interesting information, highlight key concepts, and review content so that you can solidify your understanding of the exam's concepts. Test your knowledge with sample questions and detailed answer explanations in the text that help you think through the problems on the exam and two full-length practice tests that reflect the content and format of the ELA. We're pleased you've chosen Cirrus to be a part of your professional journey.

Terms

active listening

adjective

listening that is focused and empathetic

a word that modifies a noun or pronoun

advanced fluency stage of
language acquisition

adverb

affixes

learners demonstrate near-native ability and use complex, multiphrase and multiclause sentences to convey their ideas

a word that modifies an adjective, adverb, verb, phrase, or clause

added to words or roots to change their meanings; include prefixes (added to the beginning of a word or root) and suffixes (added to the end of a word or root)

allusion

analytic rubrics

analyzing text organization

a reference to a historical person or event, a fictional character or event, a mythological or religious character or event, or an artist or artistic work

break the assignment down so that points are assigned by component part

analyzing how a text is organized in order to better comprehend an author's purpose for writing

assonance

audience

ballad

the inclusion of words with the same vowel sounds within one or two lines of poetry

the reader/readers

a short narrative song about an event that is considered important

canon

central idea

character analysis

a group of works that are considered to be culturally, artistically, or historically significant

the basic underlying idea of informational text

understanding the role of a character in a story via the character's actions, traits, relationships, and personality

citations

clause

climax

used in a research paper to show the resources and reference materials where information originated

a group of words with both a subject and a predicate

turning point during which the conflict reaches a crisis point

cognition

collaborative writing

communicative competence

the mental processes of understanding, reasoning, and knowing

when partners or small groups of students work together to complete segments of a writing process (or the full process) together

being able to speak a language appropriately in a social context and correctly in terms of rules and structure

complex sentence

compound sentence

compound-complex sentence

a sentence made up of an independent clause and one or more dependent clauses

a sentence made up of two independent clauses (or simple sentences)

a sentence that has two or more independent clauses and one or more dependent clauses

conclusion

conjunction

connotation

leaves the reader with a sense of closure by reiterating the author's thesis and sometimes providing a summary of his or her main points

joins words into phrases, clauses, and sentences

the intended meaning of a word beyond its literal meaning

constructivism

context

conversational language

as readers become involved with a text, they construct meaning through an active process of integrating what they are reading with their own reactions, knowledge, beliefs, and ideas

the historical and cultural time in which a text was written

familiar and informal language

credibility

denotation

descriptive writing

proof of the reliability of a source

the literal meaning of a word

a writing style that emphasizes the production of imagery using words and figurative language that appeal to the reader's five senses

dialect

dramatic irony

dystopian fiction

language that is particular to a geographical location or consolidated social group

when the audience knows about something of which a character or characters are not aware

explores social, cultural, and political structures in the context of a unpleasant futuristic world

early production stage of language acquisition

ethos

expository writing

learners produce single-word and two- to three-word phrases and can respond to questions and statements

ethical appeals

a writing style that explains an idea or concept or informs the reader about a topic

fables

falling action

figurative language

short stories intended to teach moral lessons

events that move the characters away from the conflict and into a new life

language that conveys images and ideas separate from the actual meanings of the words used

first-person point of view

fluency

formative assessments

one character tells the story from his or her direct experience using pronouns such as *I*, *my*, *mine*, and *we*

the ability to read with ease and automaticity

assignments given leading up to the summative assessments, which the teacher uses to evaluate student progress and adjust instruction

free verse

genre

grammar

poetry without patterns of rhyme or regular meter

type of a text (e.g., poetry, drama, picture book, graphic novel, folktale, myth, fairy tale, tall tale, historical fiction, science fiction)

the way parts of speech work together in sentences and how words are grouped to make meaning such as in phrases or clauses

haiku

high frequency letter-sound
correspondences

holistic rubrics

a short poem format, created in Japan, that consists of three lines and seventeen syllables divided into five, seven, and five between the lines

letter-sound correspondences that occur most often in the English language

provide a grade based on the overall effectiveness of the product

identifying point of view

inferences

interjection

using genre and pronoun clues to identify who is telling a story to best form accurate conclusions about the events of the story

conclusions about what an author suggests in a text based on context clues

a word that expresses emotion

intermediate fluency stage of language acquisition

introduction

letter-sound correspondence

learners are able to speak in more complex sentences and catch and correct many of their errors

sets the tone, topic, direction, style, and mood for the writing that is to follow

the relationship between the spoken sounds in words and the printed letters that correspond to those sounds

levels of language proficiency

literal

logical fallacy

L1) entering, L2) beginning, L3) developing, L4) expanding, and L5) bridging

the most basic or exact meaning of a word

an error or breakdown in logical reasoning

logos

mechanics

metacognition

logical appeals

---

the conventions of print that are not necessary in spoken language, such as punctuation, capitalization, and indentation (spelling is a component of mechanics but is treated as a separate category in elementary school)

---

readers thinking about what they are thinking as they read so that they can recognize immediately any confusion or uncertainty

metaphor

meter

misplaced modifier

a type of figurative language that describes something that may be unfamiliar to the reader (the topic) by referring to it as though it were something else that is more familiar to the reader (the vehicle)

the basic rhythmic structure of the lines or verses in poetry

a modifier that causes confusion because it does not modify its intended word or phrase

Modern Period (American)

modifiers

moral

1900 – 1950

Writers wrote about the world wars, alienation, the Roaring Twenties, the Depression, and the changing world.

F. Scott Fitzgerald (*The Great Gatsby*); John Steinbeck (*The Grapes of Wrath, Of Mice and Men*); Richard Wright (*Black Boy*); the poetry of Robert Frost, Nikki Giovanni, and E. E. Cummings; the stories of Katherine Porter, Flannery O'Connor, Alice Walker, Sinclair Lewis, and Eudora Welty; the plays of Tennessee Williams, August Wilson, and Eugene O'Neil; the speeches and letters of Malcolm X and Martin Luther King

words or phrases that change the meanings of or add details to other words or phrases in a sentence

the lesson the author intends to teach the reader in a literary text

morphemes

myths

narrative poems

the smallest units of language that contain meaning

stories, often involving gods or demigods, that attempt to explain certain practices or phenomena

poems that tell stories

narrative writing

noun

onset

a writing style that tells a personal or fictional story that entertains the reader

a person, place, thing, or idea

the beginning consonant or consonant blend of a syllable

overwriting

paraphrase

pathos

when a writer uses inappropriately and awkwardly ornate language or complex, technical terms

changing both the wording and the syntax used to express an idea

emotional appeals

persuasive writing

phoneme

phoneme blending

a writing style that convinces, or persuades, a reader to subscribe to the author's opinion or point of view (often used for speeches and advertisements)

each small unit of sound in a language

combining phonemes to make a word

phoneme deletion

phoneme segmentation

phoneme substitution

removing phonemes from words to make new words

separating phonemes in words

replacing phonemes in words to make new words

phonemic awareness

phonics

phrase

a type of phonological awareness; an understanding of how phonemes form a language by creating differences in the meanings of words

the study of the relationship between the spoken sounds in words and the printed letters that correspond to those sounds

a group of words with either a subject or a predicate

phonological awareness

pidgin

plagiarism

an understanding of how sounds, syllables, words, and word parts can be orally manipulated to break apart words, make new words, and create rhymes

a grammatically simplified mode of communicating that may use elements of more than one language

intentionally copying and taking credit for another person's work

plays

plot development

preposition

dramatic works meant to be performed on a stage

the exposition, rising action, problem/climax, falling action, and resolution

describes relationships in time and space

preproduction stage of language acquisition

primary sources

process writing

the silent period; learners refrain from speaking but will listen, may copy words down, and can respond to visual cues

original materials representative of an event, experience, place, or time period

instructing students in the use of a clear process for writing and in the use of techniques and strategies for completing each part of the process

pronoun

proofreading

prosody

a word that replaces a noun

checking a final draft for typos

the range of vocal expressions a reader uses when reading aloud, including rhythm, intonation, and stress patterns

punctuation

qualitative measures

quantitative measures

periods, commas, question marks, exclamation marks, and other markings that divide text or help a reader know when to change pace or read with inflection

contributors to text leveling that include analysis of text elements such as structure, language clarity, and knowledge demands

contributors to text leveling that include readability scores determined by computer algorithms that evaluate text elements such as word frequency and sentence length

reader and task considerations

reading accuracy

reading rate

matching texts to particular students, classes, and/or tasks based on their inherent needs as determined by the professional judgment of educators

the ability to recognize or decode words correctly

the speed and fluidity with which a reader can read

Realistic Period

Renaissance Period

register

1855 – 1910

Writers sought to portray American life as it truly was and emphasized verisimilitude (likeness to life). The Realistic Period included Civil War writers, Regionalists, and Naturalists.

Mary Chestnut (*Diary of Mary Chestnut),* Frederick Douglass (*My Bondage and My Freedom),* Willa Cather (*My Antonia),* William Faulkner (*Absalom! Absalom!),* Jack London (*Cry of the Wild*), Stephen Crane (*The Red Badge of Courage)*

1485 – 1660

Included the Elizabethan Age of great English drama and public theatres; writers were interested in love and in the nature of human beings.

the poetry of Christopher Marlowe and Edmund Spenser; the works of William Shakespeare

particular styles of language determined by purpose, audience, and social context

reliable sources

rhyme scheme

rime

trustworthy materials that come from experts in the field of study

rhyme pattern in a poem; may be represented as letters (e.g., *abab*, *aabb*, *aabba*)

a syllable's vowel and its remaining consonants (not including the onset)

Romantic Period (British)

roots

rubric

1785 – 1830

Writers believed that truth was found in nature and unrestrained imaginative experience; many poems and lyrical ballads were written, as well as imaginative gothic horror novels.

the poetry of William Wordsworth, John Keats, Lord Byron, and Percy Bysshe Shelley; Samuel Taylor Coleridge ("The Rime of the Ancient Mariner"); Mary Shelley (*Frankenstein)*

the basis of many words in the English language, typically derived from Latin or Greek

assessment tools that teachers use to objectively assign scores to projects or assignments whose merits are difficult to quantify, especially writing assignments

satire

schemas

second-person point of view

a text that uses critical humor to reveal vice and foolishness in individuals and institutions

cognitive connections that are molded in an individual's mind over time

a narrative perspective from an external "you," whether that be the reader or unknown other

secondary sources

setting

sight words

sources that inform about events, experiences, places, or time periods using primary sources but that were not directly involved in the event in any way

where a story takes place

words that are repeated most often in text

silent period

simile

simple sentence

the preproduction stage of language acquisition

a type of figurative language that directly points to similarities between two things

a sentence that contains a subject, a verb, and a completed thought

situational irony

Socratic seminar

soliloquy

when something happens that contradicts what the audience expected to happen

a teaching technique in which a leader prompts discussion solely by asking questions and allowing the class to share and then respond to and build upon one another's ideas

a monologue delivered as if nobody is listening

sonnet

speech emergence stage of language acquisition

stages of language acquisition

a lyrical poem composed of fourteen lines, usually written in iambic pentameter

learners can chunk simple words and phrases into sentences that may or may not be grammatically correct and can understand simple readings when reinforced by graphics or pictures

preproduction, early production, speech emergence, interme-diate fluency, and advanced fluency

stanza

structural analysis

summarization

a group of lines in a poem followed by a space

an analysis of the roots and affixes of words

distilling and condensing a text into its main idea and key details by identifying story elements

summative assessments

syllables

syntax

assignments (tests and exams) that are intended to assess a student's overall mastery of a long-term objective

phonological units composed of onsets and rimes that can be blended, substituted, segmented, and deleted like phonemes

the grammatical formations and patterns of sentences

text features

text leveling

text structure

supplemental information outside of the main text such as chapter headings, titles, sidebars (boxes of explanatory or additional information set aside from main text) and hyperlinks

complexity of text as determined by quantitative measures, qualitative measures, and reader and task considerations

organizational structures like cause and effect, problem and solution, sequence of events or steps-in-a-process, compare and contrast, and description

theme

think-pair-shares

third-person limited omniscient
point of view

the basic idea that the author wants to convey in a literary text

an activity in which students have the opportunity to first share briefly with a partner before sharing their responses with the whole class

a narrative perspective in which a detached narrator tells the story from one character's point of view, including that character's internal thoughts and feelings

third-person objective point of view

third-person omniscient point of view

tone

a narrative perspective in which a detached narrator relates the actions and dialogue of the story, but not the thoughts or feelings of any characters

a narrative perspective in which a detached and all-knowing narrator tells the story from the point of view of all of the characters, including all of their thoughts and feelings

the author's attitude toward the reader and toward the subject of the text

unreliable sources

usage

verb

untrustworthy materials from a person or institution that does not have the educational background, expertise, or evidence of legitimate sources to support a claim

common rules for how language is used under certain conditions or within particular styles

a word that expresses action or being

verbal irony

villanelle

World Literature

when a character or narrator says something that is the opposite of what he or she means

a poem that is usually nineteen lines long; it has five stanzas, each with three lines, and a final stanza of four lines

can refer to all national literatures, but the term usually refers to a group of important representative literary works that are circulated and studied around the globe

The Epic of Gilgamesh (the Fertile Crescent), *The Odyssey*, Greek tragedies, *The Tale of Genji* (Japan), *Journey to the West* (China),

Grammar

What is the difference between a proper noun and a common noun?

Are the words *am*, *is*, and *are* verbs? Why or why not?

A proper noun is capitalized; it names a certain person, place, or thing. Examples: Barack Obama, Los Angeles, the Rock of Gibraltar. A common noun is usually not capitalized; it names more than one person, place, or thing. Examples: captain, highway, boulder.

Yes, they are "verbs of being," forms of the verb *to be*. Not all verbs express action.

What is a proper adjective?

Name three of the seven coordinating conjunctions.

Which two words in the following sentence are prepositions?

My cat usually sleeps on the bed with me.

It is a capitalized adjective that refers to a certain person, place, or thing, and modifies a noun. Examples: in the term *African American*, *African* is a proper adjective that modifies the proper noun *American*; in the term *Belgian waffle*, *Belgian* is a proper adjective that modifies the common noun *waffle*.

and, or, but, nor, so, for, yet

on and *with*

Which word in the following sentence is an interjection?

Wow, what is that horrible smell?

How can you tell if a sentence is complete?

Which words in the following sentence form an adjective phrase?

The woman on the bus wore a uniform.

Wow

A complete sentence expresses a complete thought. It contains at least one subject (a noun or noun phrase) and at least one predicate (a verb or verb phrase).

"On the bus" is an adjective phrase that modifies the noun *woman*.

Which words in the following sentence form a dependent clause (also known as a subordinate clause)?

When it started to rain, we ran indoors.

What is the purpose of a declarative sentence, and with what punctuation mark does it usually end?

What is the main difference between a comma and a semicolon?

"When it started to rain"

A declarative sentence (like this one) makes a statement; it usually ends with a period.

A comma indicates a short pause, and a semicolon indicates a longer pause. In a compound sentence, a semicolon can take the place of a comma followed by a conjunction. Example: *My cat has annoying habits; for example, she likes to sit in front of my computer screen.*

What is wrong with the expression "I could care less"?

What is wrong with the following sentence?

Excellent movies, such as Cocoon, Parenthood, *and* Apollo 13 *reveals director Ron Howard's gift for portraying life in the United States.*

How can a run-on sentence be corrected?

The correct expression is "I *couldn't* care less." It means "I don't care at all." If you *could* care less about something, then you *do* care about it.

The singular verb *reveals* does not agree with its plural subject, *movies*. The verb should be changed to *reveal*.

A run-on sentence can be fixed by 1) inserting a comma and a conjunction; 2) inserting a semicolon; or 3) rewriting the run-on sentence as two sentences.

Read this sentence and identify the misspelled word or words.

Their standing right over there with they're parents.

In the sentence *I threw the ball to Pablo*, which pronoun could you substitute for Pablo's name?

Carrying a heavy backpack, I walked up the steep, dusty trail in 90-degree weather.

What verb could you substitute for *walked* to make the sentence more descriptive?

The first word in the sentence, *Their*, should be spelled *They're* (or *They are*). The second-to-last word, *they're*, should be spelled *their*.

him

Examples: *hiked, trudged, tramped, plodded, slogged*

What are the main differences between adjectives and adverbs?

In the following sentence, is the word *because* a coordinating conjunction or a subordinating conjunction?

I dislike fresh tomatoes because they have a squishy texture.

In the phrase "lying peacefully on the comfortable couch," which word is a preposition?

An adjective modifies a noun or a pronoun. Examples: *a gorgeous sunset*; *she is courageous*. An adverb modifies a verb, an adjective, or another adverb. Examples: *to amble lazily*; *amazingly beautiful*; *to speak incredibly quietly*.

Because is a subordinating conjunction; it introduces a subordinate clause ("because they have a squishy texture") and connects it to the sentence's main clause ("I dislike fresh tomatoes").

on

Which word in the following sentence is an interjection?

As I lay there, I thought to myself, hey, aren't I supposed to be somewhere at noon today?

Which word or words in this sentence form a direct object?

I quickly read the third chapter.

Which words in the following sentence form an adverb phrase?

While I was running around Green Lake, I saw Gary Grenell, a local photographer.

hey

chapter or "the third chapter"

"around Green Lake"

Which words in the following sentence form the main clause (also known as an independent clause)?

Although I like uncooked raisins, I do not like them in cookies, cinnamon rolls, or hot cereal.

What is the purpose of an interrogative sentence, and with what punctuation mark does this type of sentence end?

Which punctuation mark in the following sentence could be replaced by a colon (:)?

Let me tell you something important— never carry your Social Security number in your wallet!

"I do not like them in cookies, cinnamon rolls, or hot cereal."

An interrogative sentence asks a question; it ends with a question mark.

The em dash could be replaced by a colon, as seen in the following sentence.

Let me tell you something important: never carry your Social Security number in your wallet!

What is wrong with the
following sentence?

*I am so excited about this project that my
head is literally exploding with ideas.*

What is wrong with the
following sentence?

*My mom, my sister, and even my dad enjoys
cooking huge family dinners on weekends.*

What is a comma splice, and how can it
be corrected?

The adverb *literally* means "actually, really, in fact." You can't truthfully say your head is "literally exploding" unless it is *actually* exploding (in which case you probably wouldn't be able to say or write anything).

The singular verb *enjoys* does not agree with its plural subject, "my mom, my sister, and even my dad." The verb should be changed to *enjoy*.

A comma splice is an incorrectly-written compound sentence in which there is a comma but no conjunction connecting two shorter complete sentences. A comma splice can be fixed by 1) inserting a conjunction after the comma, 2) replacing the comma with a semicolon, or 3) rewriting the sentence as two sentences.

Read this sentence, identify the misspelled word, and spell it correctly.

I was surprised to find that in the past year, my younger cousin has grown taller then I am.

Complete the following sentence with *one* pronoun.

_____ all live together at 2145 Basil Lane.

In the following sentence, which verb has a direct object? Which one or two words comprise the direct object?

Purring loudly, the mother cat grooms her kittens with her rough tongue.

The third-to-last word, *then*, should be spelled *than*.

We or *They*

The verb *grooms* has a direct object: *kittens* or "her kittens." (The verb *purring* does not have a direct object.)

In the following sentence, identify one adverb and one adjective.

Sleeping on the floor can be amazingly comfortable.

In the sentence *I like baked potatoes, but I love French fries*, is the word *but* a coordinating conjunction or a subordinating conjunction?

Identify two prepositional phrases in the following sentence.

My family and I used to camp in the Wawona Campground at Yosemite National Park.

Adverb: *amazingly*; adjective: *comfortable*

But is a coordinating conjunction; it connects two short—but complete—sentences. ("I like baked potatoes" and "I love French fries"). Neither short sentence is a subordinate clause.

1) "in the Wawona Campground; 2) "at Yosemite National Park"

**Which one of these words is NOT
an interjection?**
hey, wow, oh, painful, hooray, ouch

**Which two words in this sentence form
the sentence's subject?**
Thinking aloud may not be wise.

**Which word in the following sentence is a
helping verb? Also identify the verb that
the helping verb "helps."**
Might you need help from Matty and me?

The word *painful* is an adjective, not an interjection.

"Thinking aloud"

The helping verb is *might*; it "helps" (modifies) the verb *need*, as in "you <u>might need</u> help."

Which words in the following sentence form the main clause (independent clause), and which form the subordinate clause (dependent clause)?

While I would love to attend the conference, the decision is up to my supervisor.

What is the purpose of an exclamation, and with what punctuation mark does this type of sentence usually end?

What punctuation mark is missing from the following sentence, and where does the missing mark belong?

My mom stared at me and exclaimed, "You have got to be kidding!

The main clause is: "the decision is up to my supervisor." The subordinate clause is: "While I would love to attend the conference."

An exclamation expresses strong emotion; it usually ends with an exclamation mark. Example: *Wow, I just love riding on rollercoasters!*

The sentence is missing a closing quotation mark; it belongs at the very end of the sentence, after the exclamation mark.

The following sentence might work fine in an informal conversation or a friendly email. However, it uses language that is inappropriate for formal writing. How might you restate the following to make it sound more formal?

Addy was all like, "Shut UP! Are you serious?"

What is wrong with the following sentence?

That is a flimsy explanation which do not adequately excuse their actions.

What is a rambling sentence? Is a rambling sentence always ungrammatical?

Addy was amazed when I told her the news. She said, "I can't believe it! Are you sure it's true?"

The plural helping verb *do* does not agree with its singular subject, *explanation*. *Do* should be replaced with *does*.

A rambling sentence is one that goes on and on in a tedious way; it is impossible to read aloud in one breath. Not all rambling sentences are ungrammatical.

Identify two misspelled words and spell them correctly.

Why didn't you tell me that your leaving on a two-week visit to you're grandmother?

Complete the following sentence with *one* pronoun.

I hope my grandparents will be in shape for their bicycle trip this summer—I don't want them to injure _____.

In the following sentence, which verb has an indirect object? Which one or two words comprise the indirect object?

I yawned, stretched, scratched a mosquito bite on my arm, and gave my dog her breakfast.

The seventh word, *your*, should be spelled *you're*. The second-to-last word, *you're*, should be spelled *your*.

themselves

The verb *gave* has an indirect object: *dog* or "my dog."

In the following sentence, identify one adverb and one adjective.

I will be everlastingly grateful to you if you do me this favor.

Although November is usually my favorite month of the year, this year it rained too much for me.

Is the word *although* a coordinating conjunction or a subordinating conjunction?

What is the purpose of an imperative sentence, and with which punctuation mark(s) does this type of sentence usually end?

Adverb: *everlastingly*; adjective: *grateful*

Although is a subordinating conjunction; it connects a subordinate clause ("Although November is usually my favorite month of the year") to the sentence's main clause ("this year it rained too much for me").

An imperative sentence is a command; it usually ends with a period or an exclamation mark. Examples: *Follow the directions at the top of your test sheet. Set the table right NOW!*

FIND THE ERROR:

Not every nation has a President as its leader; some have prime ministers, some have kings or queens, and others have military dictators.

FIND THE ERROR:

In our club, everyone who attends the meetings stay afterward to help clean up.

FIND THE ERROR:

I love French Fries, Belgian waffles, and Italian pasta.

In this sentence, *president* is a common noun (a noun that names more than one person), so it should not be capitalized.

The plural verb *stay* does not agree with its singular subject, *everyone*. *Stay* should be replaced with *stays*.

Even though the proper adjective *French* is capitalized, the common noun *fries* should be lowercased.

FIND THE ERROR:

First we will fly to Copenhagen, a port city in Denmark and then we will board a ship and sail to several different Baltic nations.

FIND THE ERROR:

Whenever I scratch my dog's belly, she grins over joy.

FIND THE ERROR:

What is that delicious—wow!—scent wafting out of the kitchen?

This compound sentence needs a comma inserted after *Denmark* and before the conjunction *and*.

The preposition *over* is incorrectly used here; it should be replaced with *with*. Alternatively, the phrase "over joy" might be replaced with *joyfully*.

The interjection *wow* is incorrectly placed in the sentence; it interrupts the sentence's flow. *Wow* should be moved to the beginning of the sentence and followed by a comma. Alternatively, this interjection could form a one-word exclamation by itself: *Wow! What is that delicious scent wafting out of the kitchen?*

FIND THE ERROR:

It is Ana's birthday next Wednesday, we're planning a family celebration for the following weekend.

FIND THE ERROR:

The two older people are Shelby's great-grandparents standing over there.

FIND THE ERROR:

I would love to attend your dinner party, my wife has made other plans for the night of the 12th.

This is an incorrectly constructed sentence (a comma splice). It needs a conjunction such as *so* or *and* following the comma and before the word *we're*.

The adjective phrase "standing over there" is misplaced in the sentence. It should be moved to follow the noun it modifies, *people*: *The two older people <u>standing over there</u> are Shelby's great-grandparents.*

This sentence is incorrectly constructed (it is a comma splice). It needs a subordinating conjunction such as *While* or *Although* at the beginning of the clause "I would love to attend your dinner party." Alternatively, the conjunction *but* could be inserted after the comma and before the word *my.*

FIND THE ERROR:

Alexander Hamilton, whose portrait is on the twenty-dollar bill, was one of our nation's "Founding Fathers"?

FIND THE ERROR:

"Wow;" she exclaimed. "This is one of the best days of my entire life!"

FIND THE ERROR:

Lydia does not agree with this president's policies, so she could care less if his approval rating drops even lower in the polls.

This is a statement (or declarative sentence), so it should end with a period, not a question mark.

The semicolon following *Wow* is incorrect punctuation. This mark should be changed to a comma or an exclamation mark.

The correct expression is "could *not* care less." "Could care less" is incorrect—it conveys the opposite meaning from the one intended.

FIND THE ERROR:

The fact that movies and TV shows based on Jane Austen's completed novels has attracted millions of viewers would have astonished the author, who died 200 years ago.

FIND THE ERROR:

Sometimes I wonder whether I will ever travel to Africa, Asia, South America, or Antarctica—so far, I have never been to any of these continents; however, I live in the United States, I have traveled to Canada and Mexico, and I have been to many nations in Europe, including England, Scotland, Ireland, France, Italy, Switzerland, and Holland.

FIND THE ERROR:

Wow, your lucky to have such a big apartment, and you're patio is so nice and shady!

The singular verb *has attracted* does not agree with its plural subject, *movies*. *Has* should be changed to *have*.

While this sentence is not ungrammatical, it is a rambling sentence and should probably be rewritten. As it stands, it is a sentence that is too long and tedious to read.

The second word, *your*, should be spelled *you're* or "you are." The eleventh word, *you're*, should be spelled *your*.

FIND THE ERROR:

Which State in the United States is larger, Alaska or Texas?

FIND THE ERROR:

Katrina, the youngest of my four cats, are due for a check-up at the vet.

FIND THE ERROR:

You have two choices: you can work overtime to finish the project, and you can tell your supervisor that you cannot meet the deadline.

The second word in the sentence, *State*, should be lowercased; here it functions as a common noun, not as a proper noun.

The plural verb *are* does not agree with its singular subject, *Katrina*. *Are* should be changed to *is*.

The conjunction *and* should be changed to *or* to indicate a choice; as is, the sentence does not make sense.

FIND THE ERROR:

Alex plans to buy the most big cake he can find for his sister's birthday.

FIND THE ERROR:

We had made an appointment to meet at 2 p.m., so by 2:30 p.m. I began to wonder where Amy was at.

FIND THE ERROR:

Danny stepped on a tack and yelled, "Ouch?" as it pierced his heel.

The superlative form of the adjective *big* is *biggest*, not "most big."

The preposition *at* should be deleted from the end of the sentence; it is not needed.

The question mark following the interjection *Ouch* should be changed to an exclamation mark to show strong emotion (in this case, pain).

FIND THE ERROR:

Can you run to the grocery store tomorrow and pick up some milk and we need eggs, too.

FIND THE ERROR:

On the test people who don't carefully read and follow directions are likely to make mistakes.

FIND THE ERROR:

I can get eight hours of sleep tonight, I don't think I will be able to get up early enough to drive to the city in time for the meeting.

This is a run-on sentence. It can be corrected in more than one way. Two examples: *Can you run to the grocery store tomorrow and pick up some milk and eggs? Can you run to the grocery store tomorrow and pick up some milk? We need eggs, too.*

As is, this sentence is unclear. The phrase "on the test" is meant to modify the noun *mistakes*, so the phrase should be moved to follow this noun: *People who don't carefully read and follow directions are likely to make mistakes on the test.*

This sentence is incorrectly constructed (it is a comma splice), and it does not make sense as is. It needs the subordinating conjunction *Unless* at the beginning of the clause "I can get eight hours of sleep tonight." Alternatively, "I can" might be changed to "If I don't" or "If I cannot."

FIND THE ERROR:
Are you coming with us to Carmina's party this Saturday night.

FIND THE ERROR:
My grandma says that "when she was in high school, she and her classmates handwrote or typed their essays— desktop computers were not common until the late 1980s."

FIND THE ERROR:
I ate so much food on Thanksgiving that my stomach was literally bursting at the seams.

This is a question (or interrogative sentence), so it should end with a question mark, not a period.

This is not a direct quotation, so the quotation marks should be deleted from this sentence. (The speaker is paraphrasing his or her grandmother.)

Since human stomachs do not have seams like clothing or cloth toys, this sentence describes an impossible (and horrifying) scenario. Deleting the word *literally* would make it clear that the writer is using the term "bursting at the seams" figuratively.

FIND THE ERROR:

Only one among the school's 450 students were invited to enter the city's annual spelling bee.

FIND THE ERROR:

Thinking about all the happy and not-so-happy memories from my years in elementary and middle school.

FIND THE ERROR:

For some reason, my family has always ended up living in neighborhoods where most of the other residents own newer, shinier cars then we do.

The plural helping verb *were* does not agree with its singular subject, *one. Were* should be changed to *was*.

This is a sentence fragment. One way to complete the sentence might be the following: *That night, as I was falling asleep, I started thinking about all the happy and not-so-happy memories from my years in elementary and middle school.*

The third-to-last word, *then,* should be spelled *than*.

FIND THE ERROR:

Our generous grandparents gave my twin sister and I brand-new bicycles for our birthday.

FIND THE ERROR:

After Mario had camped out in a tent for two weeks, his mattress at home felt delicious soft, and his sheets felt wondrously smooth and clean.

FIND THE ERROR:

In your opinion, which dress is more pretty, the blue silk one or the magenta satin one?

The subject pronoun *I* should be changed to the object pronoun *me*.

The adjective *delicious* should be changed to *deliciously*, an adverb (which modifies the adjective *soft*).

The comparative form of the adjective *pretty* is *prettier*, not "more pretty."

FIND THE ERROR:
I was full after eating a big breakfast, so I ate a huge midmorning snack and a gigantic lunch.

FIND THE ERROR:
No one beside me volunteered to serve on the clean-up committee.

FIND THE ERROR:
Hey who's that knocking on our front door?

The coordinating conjunction *so* does not make sense in this compound sentence. Substituting *yet* or *but* for *so* would clarify the writer's meaning. Alternatively, the sentence could be rewritten as follows: *Even though I was full after eating a big breakfast, I ate a huge midmorning snack and a gigantic lunch.*

Beside is a preposition that means "next to," so it does not make sense here. This word should be changed to besides, a preposition that means "except or in addition to." Alternatively, *beside* could be changed to *except*.

The interjection *Hey* should be followed by a comma. Alternatively, the interjection could form its own one-word exclamation: *Hey! Who's that knocking on our front door?*

FIND THE ERROR:

On Friday nights we usually stay home and watch a movie, we sometimes munch on snacks, such as popcorn.

FIND THE ERROR:

From one rooftop to the neighboring one, without pausing to think, to escape the fire, Ben leapt.

FIND THE ERROR:

My movie club meets on Tuesdays, I cannot sign up for a Tuesday/Thursday computer class.

This is a comma splice. It can be corrected in more than one way. Two examples: *On Friday nights we usually stay home, watch a movie, and munch on snacks, such as popcorn. On Friday nights we usually stay home and watch a movie; often we munch on snacks, such as popcorn.*

There are three adverb phrases in this sentence; all three modify the verb *leapt*. If the sentence is to make proper sense, the phrases must be reordered. For example: *To escape the fire, without pausing to think, Ben leapt from one rooftop to the neighboring one.*

This sentence is incorrectly constructed (it is a comma splice). The sentence needs a subordinating conjunction such as *Since* or *Because* at the beginning of the clause "my movie club meets on Tuesdays." Alternatively, the coordinating conjunction *so* could be inserted after the comma and before the pronoun *I*.

FIND THE ERROR:

After you clear the table, please rinse the dishes and load them into
the dishwasher?

FIND THE ERROR:

Here's what I'd like you to do, tidy up the living room, dust the furniture, and vacuum the rug.

FIND THE ERROR:

To many people, promptness and respect for others are one in the same.

This is a command (or imperative sentence), so it should end with a period, not a question mark.

The first comma in the sentence should be replaced with a colon (:).

The correct expression is "one <u>and</u> the same," not "one <u>in</u> the same."

FIND THE ERROR:

Almost all of the people in my family was planning to attend the reunion.

FIND THE ERROR:

Holly, the woman who works in the front office.

FIND THE ERROR:

There aunt is standing right over there with their parents.

The singular helping verb *was* does not agree with its plural subject, *people. Was* should be changed to *were.*

This is a sentence fragment. One way to complete the sentence might be the following: *Holly, the woman who works in the front office, is helpful and friendly to everyone who visits our workplace.*

The first word, *There,* should be spelled *Their* to show possession.

FIND THE ERROR:

I usually give birthday gifts to she and Jacqueline.

FIND THE ERROR:

All my animals—including my forty-pound dog—usually sleeps on my bed at night.

FIND THE ERROR:

The bumblebee bat is the most tiny mammal in the world.

The subject pronoun *she* should be changed to the object pronoun *her*.

The singular verb *sleeps* does not agree with its plural subject, *animals*. *Sleeps* should be changed to *sleep*.

The superlative form of the adjective *tiny* is *tiniest*, not "most tiny."

FIND THE ERROR:

Whether we were unable to attend the wedding, we sent Mikki and her husband a wedding gift.

FIND THE ERROR:

Wow, that was the most incredible performance I've ever seen.

The coordinating conjunction *Whether* does not make sense in this sentence. Substituting *Although* would clarify the writer's meaning. Alternatively, the sentence could be rewritten as follows: *We were unable to attend the wedding, but we sent Mikki and her husband a wedding gift anyhow.*

This is an exclamation (or an exclamatory sentence), so it should end with an exclamation mark, not a period.

Reading

When the Spanish-American War broke out in 1898, the U.S. Army was small and understaffed. President William McKinley called for 1,250 volunteers primarily from the Southwest to serve in the First U.S. Volunteer Calvary. Eager to fight, the ranks were quickly filled by a diverse group of cowboys, gold prospectors, hunters, gamblers, Native Americans, veterans, police officers, and college students looking for an adventure.

Use context to define the word *prospectors*.

Hand washing is one of our simplest and most powerful weapons against infection. The idea behind hand washing is deceptively simple. Many illnesses are spread when people touch infected surfaces, such as door handles or other people's hands, and then touch their own eyes, mouths, or noses. So, if pathogens can be removed from the hands before they spread, infections can be prevented.

How does frequent handwashing lessen the chance that people will transfer pathogens to their own eyes, mouths, or noses?

Gold prospectors are people who search for gold, so a prospector must be an explorer who searches for gold or another precious natural substance.

When people touch surfaces such as door handles, they can pick up pathogens that others have left there. However, handwashing can remove pathogens before a person touches his own eyes, mouth, or nose. In this case, he will not become infected.

One of the reasons the flu has historically been so deadly is the amount of time between when people become infectious and when they develop symptoms. Viral shedding—the process by which the body releases viruses that have been successfully reproducing during the infection—takes place two days after infection, while symptoms do not usually develop until the third day of infection. Thus, infected individuals have at least twenty-four hours in which they may unknowingly infect others.

What happens after infection occurs but before flu symptoms develop?

During the 1920s in the United States, musicians flocked to cities such as New York and Chicago, which would become famous hubs for jazz musicians. Ella Fitzgerald, for example, moved from Virginia to New York City to begin her much-lauded singing career, and jazz pioneer Louis Armstrong got his big break in Chicago.

What did Ella Fitzgerald and Louis Armstrong have in common?

Activity level has a significant impact on a patient's energy needs. A bedridden patient will obviously expend fewer calories and thus will need to eat fewer. An elderly, bedridden women can need as little as 8.5 calories per pound of body weight: if such a patient weighed 135 pounds, she would need only 1150 calories a day.

What causes a bedridden patient to need fewer calories per day than she would need if she were not bedridden?

Viral shedding occurs two days after infection and one day before flu symptoms develop.

Both were 1920s jazz musicians who became famous when performing in big U.S. cities such as New York and Chicago.

Someone who stays in bed all the time is less active than someone who is not bedridden. The less active someone is, the fewer calories she needs.

Examples of symbiotic relationships (long-term interspecies interactions) can easily be seen in any ecosystem. In mutualism, both individuals benefit. Pollination, for example, is mutualistic—pollinators get nutrients from the flower, and the plant is able to reproduce. A relationship where one individual benefits and the other is harmed is known as parasitism. Tapeworms, which steal nutrients from their host, are parasitic.

Use context to define the term *parasitism*. Give an example of this kind of relationship.

Archaeologists have discovered the oldest known specimens of bedbugs in a cave in Oregon where humans once lived. The three different species date back to between 5,000 and 11,000 years ago. The finding gives scientists a clue as to how bedbugs became human parasites. These bedbugs, like those that plague humans today, originated as bat parasites. Scientists hypothesize that it was the co-habitation of humans and bats in the caves that encouraged the bugs to begin feeding on the humans.

What happened after humans began sleeping in caves where bats lived?

Between November 15 and December 21, 1864, Major General William Tecumseh Sherman marched Union troops from the recently captured city of Atlanta to the port of Savannah. The goal was not only to capture the port city and secure Georgia for the Union, but also to destroy the Confederacy's infrastructure and demoralize its people.

Where did General Sherman and his troops begin marching on November 15?

Parasitism is a symbiotic relationship in which "one individual benefits and the other is harmed." For example, a tapeworm benefits from its relationship with its host, but the host suffers (since the worm "steals" a portion of the host's nutrients).

After humans began sleeping in caves, species that originated as bat parasites became human parasites as well. Eventually, humans named such parasites "bedbugs."

Atlanta, Georgia; the text says that they marched "from the recently captured city of Atlanta to the port of Savannah."

It seemed to Julia as if the other drivers on the road felt as sluggish and surly as as she did—it took her an extra fifteen minutes to get to work. And when she arrived, all the parking spots were full. By the time she'd finally found a spot in the overflow lot, she was thirty minutes late for work. She'd hoped her boss would be too busy to notice, but he'd already put a pile of paperwork on her desk with a note that simply said "Rewrite."

How does Julia know that her boss *has* noticed that she is late for work?

In 1864, marching from Atlanta to Savannah, General Sherman and his Union troops destroyed rail lines and burned buildings and fields. They packed only twenty days' worth of rations, foraging for the rest of their supplies from farms along the way. By the time they reached Savannah, they had destroyed 300 miles of railroad, countless cotton gins and mills, seized 4,000 mules, 13,000 head of cattle, 9.5 million pounds of corn, and 10.5 million pounds of fodder. Sherman estimated his troops inflicted $100 million in damages.

What did the Union troops do after using up the rations they packed?

At midnight on Saturday, August 12, 1961, units of the East German army moved into position and began closing the border between East and West Berlin. Destroying streets that ran parallel to the border to make them impassable, they installed ninety-seven miles of barbed wire and fences around West Berlin and another twenty-seven miles along the border between West and East Berlin.

Was the author's main purpose for writing this passage to inform readers or to express an opinion? Explain how you know.

He has already put a pile of paperwork on her desk, so he must have noticed that she was not there on time.

They used supplies that they "foraged" (took or stole) "from farms along the way." These supplies included cattle, corn, and fodder.

The author's main purpose is to inform readers; no opinions are expressed, only facts.

The Gatling gun, a forerunner of the modern machine gun, was an early rapid-fire spring loaded, hand-cranked weapon. In 1861, Dr. Richard J. Gatling designed the gun to allow one person to fire many shots quickly. His goal was to reduce the death toll of war by decreasing the number of soldiers needed to fight.

Did Dr. Gatling's gun probably "reduce the death toll of war"? Why or why not?

The energy needs of patients can vary widely. Generally, energy needs are directly related to a person's weight and inversely related to age; it's also generally true that men require more calories than women. Thus, a thirty-five-year-old woman who weighs 135 pounds will require around 1800 calories a day, while an older woman would require fewer, and a heavier woman would require more. A man of the same age and weight would require 2000 calories a day.

If a sixty-year-old woman who weighs 135 pounds eats 1,800 or more calories a day, what will probably happen?

In December of 1944, Germany launched its last major offensive campaign of World War II, pushing through the dense forests of the Ardennes region of Belgium, France, and Luxembourg. Due to troop positioning, the Americans bore the brunt of the attack, incurring 100,000 deaths, the highest number of casualties of any battle during the war. However, after a month of grueling fighting in the bitter cold, a lack of fuel and a masterful American military strategy resulted in an Allied victory that sealed Germany's fate.

How did a lack of fuel "result in an Allied victory"?

No, probably not: his gun could kill more enemy soldiers in a shorter time. Also, its invention led to the creation of the "modern machine gun," which could kill an even greater number of people in an even shorter time.

She will probably gain weight. The passage says that "an older woman [who weighs 135 pounds] would require fewer [calories per day than 1,800]."

The Germans lacked fuel and so could not move their troops and equipment around efficiently. This and "a masterful American military strategy" allowed the Allies to win.

The cisco, a foot-long freshwater fish native to the Great Lakes, had almost died out by the 1950s, but today it thrives. The cisco have an invasive species, quagga mussels, to thank for their return. Quagga mussels depleted nutrients in the lakes, harming other species highly dependent on these nutrients. Cisco, however, thrive in low-nutrient environments. As other species—many invasive—diminished, cisco flourished in their place.

How did quagga mussels prevent the cisco's extinction?

One myth that prevents the advancement of pain management practices is the myth that pain is a necessary part of an animal's recovery. While some veterinarians believe that pain may prevent a healing dog, for example, from playing too vigorously, Dr. Debbie Grant says this is simply not the case. In fact, restlessness and dis-comfort may even lead to unusually high levels of agitation and may consequently slow the recovery process even further.

Regarding the idea that "pain is a necessary part of an animal's recovery," how does Dr. Grant's opinion differ from those of "some [other] veterinarians?

In 1953, doctors surgically removed the hippocampus of patient Henry Molaison in an attempt to stop his frequent seizures. Unexpectedly, he lost the ability to form new memories, leading to the biggest breakthrough in the science of memory. Molaison's long-term memory—of events more than a year before his surgery—was unchanged as was his ability to learn physical skills. From this, scientists learned that different types of memory are handled by different parts of the brain.

Based on the text, which part of the brain probably handles the task of forming new memories?

Quagga mussels depleted nutrients in the Great Lakes, harming species that needed them. Since the cisco thrives in low-nutrient environments, and because it now had fewer species to compete with, this freshwater fish stopped dying out and began to thrive again.

Dr. Grant thinks that this is a myth, and that "restlessness and discomfort may even lead to unusually high levels of agitation and may consequently slow the recovery process even further." The other vets "believe that pain may prevent a healing dog, for example, from playing too vigorously."

The hippocampus probably handles the task of forming new memories—after doctors removed Molaison's hippocampus, "he lost the ability to form new memories."

Scientists think it was too hot in the solar system's early days for water to condense into liquid or ice on the inner planets, so it had to be delivered—possibly by comets and water-bearing asteroids. NASA's Dawn mission is currently studying Ceres, which is the largest body in the asteroid belt between Mars and Jupiter. Researchers think Ceres might have a water-rich composition similar to some of the bodies that brought water to the three rocky, inner planets, including Earth.

How do scientists think Earth originally got its water?

The American love affair with popcorn began in 1912, when popcorn was first sold in theaters. The popcorn industry flourished during the Great Depression when it was advertised as a wholesome and economical food. Selling for five to ten cents a bag, it was a luxury that the downtrodden could afford. With the introduction of mobile popcorn machines at the World's Columbian Exposition, popcorn moved from the theater into fairs and parks.

Use context to define the word *downtrodden*.

Martin Seligman's 2011 book is titled *Flourish: A Visionary New Understanding of Happiness and Well-being.* The author's well-being theory addresses not only life satisfaction but also the extent to which one flourishes in his or her life. According to this theory, an individual's well-being is determined by—in addition to subjective experiences like positive emotions, engagement, and meaning— external factors like constructive relationships and personal achievement.

According to Seligman, which "external factors" help an individual to flourish?

They think Earth's water "had to be delivered—possibly by comets and water-bearing asteroids." They think Earth originally had no water because "it was too hot in the solar system's early days for water to condense into liquid or ice on the inner planets."

During the Great Depression, many people lost their jobs, so they were very poor. By "the downtrodden," the author must mean poor people, people who were beaten down—demoralized—by hard economic times.

"External factors like constructive relationships and personal achievement" help an individual to flourish.

"I have hitherto been very remiss, madam, in the proper attentions of a [dancing] partner here; I have not yet asked you how long you have been in Bath; whether you were ever here before; whether you have been at the Upper Rooms, the theatre, and the concert; and how you like the place altogether. I have been very negligent—but are you now at leisure to satisfy me in these particulars? If you are I will begin directly."

"You need not give yourself that trouble, sir."

Q. Use story context to define the word *particulars*.

Researchers at the University of California, Berkeley, decided to tackle an age-old problem: why shoelaces come untied. They recorded the shoelaces of a volunteer walking on a treadmill by attaching devices to record the acceleration, or g-force, experienced by the knot. The results were surprising. A shoelace knot experiences more g-force from a person walking than any rollercoaster can generate.

What is this passage mainly about?

Archaeologists have discovered the oldest known specimens of bedbugs in a cave in Oregon where humans once lived. The three species found in the Oregon caves are actually still around today, although they continue to prefer bats. Humans only lived seasonally in the Oregon cave system, however, which might explain why these insects did not fully transfer to human hosts like bedbugs elsewhere did.

Today, why do the three species of bedbugs "continue to prefer bats" to humans?

A man (addressed as "sir") asks a woman (addressed as "madam") several detailed questions. Then he asks if she is "now at leisure to satisfy [him] in these particulars." In other words, does she have time now to answer his detailed questions? Here, particulars must mean "details."

The passage is mainly about researchers who tried to figure out why shoelaces come untied. All the details in the passage support this main idea.

The bedbugs probably did not "fully transfer to human hosts" because humans did not live year-round in the caves where the bedbugs lived.

At the beginning of Philip Zimbardo's famous prison experiment, the participants, all healthy, stable, intelligent male Stanford University students, were classified as either guards or prisoners and told they would be acting their parts in a simulated prison environment for two weeks. However, after just six days, Zimbardo had to terminate the experiment because of the extreme behaviors he was witnessing in both groups: prisoners had become entirely submissive to and resentful of the guards, while the guards had become cruel and unrelenting in their treatment of the prisoners.

How did the experiment cause participants to act?

In recent years, hand sanitizers have become popular as an alternative to hand washing. These gels, liquids, and foams contain a high concentration of alcohol (usually at least 60 percent) that kills most bacteria and fungi; they can also be effective against some, but not all, viruses. There is a downside to hand sanitizer, however. Because the sanitizer isn't rinsed from hands, it only kills pathogens and does nothing to remove organic matter. So, hands "cleaned" with hand sanitizer may still harbor pathogens.

In what important way is handwashing more effective than using hand sanitizer?

When the Spanish-American War broke out in 1898, the officer corps was composed of veterans of the Civil War and the Indian Wars. With more volunteers than it could accept, the army set high standards: all the recruits had to be skilled on horseback and with guns. Consequently, they became known as the Rough Riders.

From the passage, it can be inferred that recruits needed to be "skilled on horseback" for what reason?

The ones playing prisoners became "entirely submissive to and resentful of the guards," while the ones playing guards became "cruel and unrelenting in their treatment of the prisoners."

Handwashing rinses away organic matter that may contain pathogens; since sanitizer is not rinsed from the hands, it may leave organic matter behind.

The recruits probably needed to be skilled on horseback because the soldiers would be cavalry or mounted troops.

Credit scores are used by many institutions that need to evaluate the risk of providing loans, rentals, or services to individuals. Banks use credit scores when deciding whether to hand out loans; they can also use them to determine the terms of the loan itself. Similarly, car dealers, landlords, and credit card companies will likely all access your credit report before agreeing to do business with you. Even your employer can access a modified version of your credit report.

What is this passage's main idea?

The Bastille, Paris's famous historical prison, was originally built in 1370 as a fortification, called a *bastide* in Old French, to protect the city from English invasion during the Hundred Years' War. It rose 100 feet into the air, had eight towers, and was surrounded by a moat more than eighty feet wide.

Use context to define the word *fortification* in this passage.

Five icy moons of Jupiter and Saturn show strong evidence of oceans beneath their surfaces: Ganymede, Europa and Callisto at Jupiter, and Enceladus and Titan at Saturn. Scientists using NASA's Hubble Space Telescope recently provided powerful evidence that Ganymede has a saltwater, sub-surface ocean, likely sandwiched between two layers of ice. Europa and Enceladus are each thought to have an ocean of liquid water beneath its surface in contact with mineral-rich rock.

Which moon has a saltwater ocean, in scientists' opinion, and why might scientists be interested in a saltwater ocean?

The main idea is expressed in the first sentence: "Credit scores are used by many institutions that need to evaluate the risk of providing loans, rentals, or services to individuals." The other sentences in the passage tell more about this main idea.

The passage says that the Bastille was originally a fortification meant "to protect [Paris] from English invasion," so a fortification must be a fort—a protective structure meant to keep enemies out.

Scientists think Jupiter's moon Ganymede "has a saltwater, sub-surface ocean, likely sandwiched between two layers of ice." A saltwater ocean might interest scientists because Earth has saltwater oceans.

Concerns about animal suffering have led to major changes in a variety of industries from entertainment to food production. In the field of veterinary medicine, this new line of inquiry—into whether animals experience pain and suffering the same way humans do—is especially clear when explored in the context of pain management.

What types of "major changes" might "concern about animal suffering" have led people to make in the "food production" industry?

Though positive psychology is a relatively young field within the social sciences, it has already made great strides in attracting attention from researchers and practitioners in the field. Further, it has already begun to gain popular attention, proving that it is on its way to meeting the goal that Dr. Seligman initially set out to accomplish—to have a positive impact on the lives of everyday people who might otherwise have no motivation to seek therapy.

What does the author mean by "a relatively young field"?

The Bastille, Paris's famous historical prison, was originally built in 1370 as a fortification, to protect the city from English invasion during the Hundred Years' War. In the seventeenth century, the government converted the fortress into an elite prison for upper-class felons, political disruptors, and spies. Residents of the Bastille arrived by direct order of the king and usually were left there to languish without a trial.

Use context to define the word *elite* in this passage.

Maybe the industry has made greater efforts to make sure that animals like chickens, pigs, and cows have more comfortable lives before they are slaughtered for food. Maybe the industry has tried to make methods of slaughtering animals more humane.

The author means that "positive psychology" developed recently.

The context says that the Bastille was "an elite prison for upper-class felons, political disruptors, and spies," so elite must mean "exclusive" or "high-class."

By Sunday morning, August 13, 1961, the border between East and West Berlin was completely shut down. Families woke up that morning suddenly divided, and some East Berliners with jobs in the west were unable to get to work. West Berlin was now an isolated island surrounded by a communist government hostile to its existence.

How can you tell from this passage that the border was shut down very quickly?

In the early twenty-first century, a new perspective on psychology emerged when Dr. Martin E. P. Seligman received funding to begin research into an idea that he referred to as positive psychology, a field that would be concerned with understanding the factors that contribute not to psychological distress but to an individual's ability to live a happy, fulfilling, productive life.

How was Dr. Seligman's "positive psychology" approach different from earlier methods of treating patients?

They made their appearance in the Lower Rooms; and here fortune was more favourable to our heroine. The master of the ceremonies introduced to her a very gentlemanlike young man as a partner; his name was Tilney. He seemed to be about four or five and twenty, was rather tall, had a pleasing countenance, a very intelligent and lively eye, and, if not quite handsome, was very near it. His address was good, and Catherine felt herself in high luck.

Who is "our heroine," and what happens to her in this part of the novel?

The phrase "woke up that morning suddenly divided" implies that this event occurred overnight.

Instead of focusing on "understanding the factors that contribute . . . to psychological distress," Seligman's approach focused on "an individual's ability to live a happy, fulfilling, productive life."

"Our heroine" is a young woman named Catherine; in this scene, she has the good luck to meet a "very gentlemanlike young man" named Tilney.

In 1989, almost a million Chinese university students descended on central Beijing, protesting for increased democracy and calling for the resignation of Communist Party leaders. For three weeks, they marched, chanted, and held daily vigils in the city's Tiananmen Square. The protests had widespread support in China, particularly among factory workers who cheered them on. For Westerners watching, it seemed to be the beginning of a political revolution in China.

When and where did the student protests occur?

One of the most dramatic acts of nonviolent resistance in India's movement for independence from Britain came in 1930, when independence leader Mahatma Gandhi organized a 240-mile march to the Arabian Sea. The goal of the march was to make salt from seawater, in defiance of British law. The British prohibited Indians from collecting or selling salt—a vital part of the Indian diet—requiring them instead to buy it from British merchants and pay a heavy salt tax.

Why didn't British authorities want the Indians to make, collect, or sell salt?

On November 20, 1969, about 90 people from an activist group, Indians of All Tribes, sailed to Alcatraz Island in San Francisco Bay, claiming it for all the tribes of North America. Their demands were ignored, so the group continued to occupy the island for the next 19 months, its numbers swelling up to 600 as others joined. By January of 1970, many of the original protestors had left, and on June 11, 1971 federal marshals forcibly removed the last residents.

When did the occupation begin and end, and how long did it last?

In 1989, in Tiananmen Square in central Beijing, China.

Probably because the British wanted the money they earned from selling and taxing salt; also, this may have been a way for the British to exert control over the Indian people.

It began on November 20, 1969, and ended on June 11, 1971; it lasted for about nineteen months.

The Scream of Nature by Edvard Munch is one of the world's best known and most desirable artworks. While most people think of it as a single painting, the iconic creation actually has four different versions: two paintings and two pastels. In 2012, one of the pastels earned one of the highest prices paid for an artwork at auction when it was sold for almost $120 million.

What is the difference between a painting and a pastel?

After World War I, powerful political and social forces pushed for a return to normalcy in the United States. The result was disengagement from the larger world and increased focus on American economic growth and personal enjoyment. Caught in the middle of this was a cache of American writers, raised on the values of the prewar world and frustrated with what they viewed as the superficiality and materialism of postwar American culture.

What caused people in the United States to "disengage from the larger world" and to become, in some American writers' opinions, "superficial" and "materialistic"?

In an effort to increase women's presence in government, several countries in Latin America, including Argentina, Brazil, and Mexico, have implemented legislated candidate quotas. These quotas require that at least 30 percent of a party's candidate list in any election cycle consists of women who have a legitimate chance at election. As a result, Latin America has the greatest number of female heads of government in the world, and the second highest percentage of female members of parliament after Nordic Europe.

Why does Latin America have "the greatest number of female heads of government in the world"?

A painting is an artwork made with paint applied with brushes, and a pastel is an artwork drawn with pastels, which are oily, chalky colored crayons.

Probably the negative experience of fighting overseas in World War I caused many Americans to focus on U.S. economic prosperity and on "personal enjoyment."

Because several Latin American countries have "implemented legislated candidate quotas . . . [that] require that at least 30 percent of a party's candidate list in any election cycle [to consist] of women who have a legitimate chance at election."

Tourists flock to Yellowstone National Park each year to view the geysers that bubble and erupt throughout it. What most of these tourists do not know is that these geysers are formed by a caldera, a hot crater in the earth's crust, that was created by a series of three eruptions of an ancient supervolcano. These eruptions, which began 2.1 million years ago, spewed between 1,000 to 2,450 cubic kilometers of volcanic matter at such a rate that the volcano's magma chamber collapsed, creating the craters.

What resulted from an ancient supervolcano's three eruptions?

Increasingly, companies are turning to subcontracting services rather than hiring full-time employees. This provides companies with many advantages such as greater flexibility, reduced legal responsibility to employees, and lower possibility of unionization within the company. However, it has also led to increasing confusion and uncertainty over the legal definition of employment.

Why might using subcontracting services "lower [the] possibility of unionization within [a] company"?

In 1974, scientists uncovered in Africa's Rift Valley a 3.2 million-year-old non-human hominid they nicknamed "Lucy." And, in 2013, researchers found the oldest fossil in the human ancestral line. Before this, the oldest fossil from the genus *Homo*—of which *Homo sapiens* are the only remaining species—dated only back to 2.3 million years ago, leaving a 700,000 gap between Lucy's species and the advent of humans. The new fossil dated back to 2.75 and 2.8 million years ago, pushing the appearance of humans back 400,000 years.

Name two important differences between "Lucy" and the fossil discovered in 2013.

The three eruptions caused the volcano's magma chamber to collapse. Then a "caldera, a hot crater in the earth's crust" formed in the area where Yellowstone National Park is located today. The caldera formed "geysers that bubble and erupt."

Union members likely must be full-time employees of a company. If the majority of a company's workers are subcontractors, it may be impossible to form a union.

"Lucy" was a "non-human hominid," and the fossil discovered in 2013 was "in the human ancestral line." "Lucy" was 3.2 million years old, and the 2013 fossil was about 2.8 million years old—so "Lucy" was about 400,000 years older.

Scientists believe that if they can restore northeastern Siberia's grassland, they will be able to slow climate change by slowing the thawing of the permafrost which lies beneath the tundra. Key to this undertaking is restoring the wildlife to the region, including wild horses, musk oxen, bison, and yak. Most ambitiously, the scientists hope to revive the wooly mammoth species which was key in trampling the ground and knocking down the trees, helping to keep the land free for grasses to grow.

Why does the author think scientists' "hope to revive the wooly mammoth species" is "ambitious"?

The most common way people measure body temperature is orally. A simple digital or disposable thermometer is placed under the tongue for a few minutes, and the task is done. There are many situations, however, when measuring temperature orally isn't an option. For example, when a person can't breathe through his nose, he won't be able to keep his mouth closed long enough to get an accurate reading. In these situations, it's often preferable to place the thermometer in the rectum or armpit.

In what situation is it "preferable to place the thermometer in the rectum or armpit"? Explain why.

A study of people who'd lost a high percentage of their body weight (>17%) in a short period of time found that they could not physically maintain their new weight. Scientists measured their resting metabolic rate and found that they'd need to consume only a few hundred calories a day to meet their metabolic needs. Basically, their bodies were in starvation mode and seemed to desperately hang on to each and every calorie.

Why did dieters' bodies go into "starvation mode"?

Because this species is extinct. "Reviving" it would probably be very difficult, if not impossible.

When a person cannot breathe through his nose; in this case, the patient could not "keep his mouth closed long enough to get an accurate reading."

Dieters' bodies went into "starvation mode" because they had "lost a high percentage of their body weight (>17%) in a short period of time." Apparently, when someone loses a lot of weight in a short period of time, the body "thinks" it is starving and "desperately [hangs] on to each and every calorie."

The Battle of Little Bighorn, commonly called Custer's Last Stand, was a battle between the Lakota, the Northern Cheyenne, the Arapaho, and the Seventh Calvary Regiment of the US Army. Led by war leaders Crazy Horse and Chief Gall and the religious leader Sitting Bull, the allied tribes of the Plains Indians decisively defeated their U.S. foes. Two hundred and sixty-eight U.S. soldiers were killed, including General George Armstrong Custer, two of his brothers, his nephew, his brother-in-law, and six Indian scouts.

What is this passage's main idea?

In recent decades, jazz has been associated with New Orleans and festivals like Mardi Gras, but in the 1920s, jazz was a booming trend whose influence reached into many aspects of American culture. In fact, the years between World War I and the Great Depression were known as the Jazz Age, a term coined by F. Scott Fitzgerald in his famous novel *The Great Gatsby*. Sometimes also called the Roaring Twenties, this period saw major urban centers experiencing new economic, cultural, and artistic vitality.

Who first called the 1920s "the Jazz Age"?

The most important part of brewing coffee is using the right water. Choose a water that you think has a nice, neutral flavor. Anything with too many minerals or contaminants will change the flavor of the coffee, and water with too few minerals won't do a good job of extracting the flavor from the coffee beans. Water should be heated to between 195 and 205 degrees Fahrenheit. Boiling water (212 degrees Fahrenheit) will burn the beans and give your coffee a scorched flavor.

What is the author's main purpose for writing this passage? How can you tell?

"The allied tribes of the Plains Indians decisively defeated their U.S. foes." All the details in the passage support this main idea.

Writer F. Scott Fitzgerald coined this term in his novel *The Great Gatsby*.

The author's main purpose is to teach readers how to make good coffee. The author furnishes detailed instructions to produce a good result.

Influenza (also called the flu) has historically been one of the most common, and deadliest, human infections. While many people who contract the virus will recover, many others will not. Over the past 150 years, tens of millions of people have died from the flu, and millions more have been left with lingering complications such as secondary infections.

Which sentence expresses this passage's main idea?

Julia's boss, Peter, had already put a pile of paperwork on her desk with a note that simply said "Rewrite." She wondered if she should point out to him that she hadn't been the one to write the reports in the first place, but decided against it. When the fire alarm went off an hour later, Julia decided she'd had enough. She grabbed her purse, and headed outside with her coworkers. She determinedly walked to her car, fired up the engine, and set a course for home.

How does Julia feel about the rewriting task?

The bacteria, fungi, insects, plants, and animals that live together in a habitat have evolved to share a pool of limited resources. They've competed for water, minerals, nutrients, sunlight, and space— sometimes for thousands or even millions of years. As these communities have evolved, the species in them have developed complex, long-term interspecies interactions known as symbiotic relationships.

What is a "symbiotic relationship"? Use context to help you define this term.

The first sentence expresses the main idea: "Influenza (also called the flu) has historically been one of the most common, and deadliest, human infections."

She thinks it is unfair of Peter to make her rewrite the reports, since she was not the person who wrote them. She does not tell Peter about her feelings, but she takes advantage of the fire alarm to go home again—this shows that she feels annoyed about having to do the task.

A symbiotic relationship between two species is a "complex, long-term interspecies interaction."

Commensalism is a relationship where one species benefits and the other is unaffected. Remoras, for instance, will attach themselves to sharks and eat the food particles they leave behind. It might seem like the shark gets nothing from the relationship, but a closer look will show that sharks in fact benefit from remoras, which clean the sharks' skin and remove parasites.

Is the relationship between sharks and remoras a good example of commensalism? Why or why not?

When done correctly, hand washing can prevent the spread of many dangerous bacteria and viruses, including those that cause the flu, the common cold, diarrhea, and many acute respiratory illnesses. The most basic method of hand washing involves only soap and water. Just twenty seconds of scrubbing with soap and a complete rinsing with water is enough to kill and/or wash away many pathogens. The process doesn't even require warm water.

Can you kill or wash away pathogens with soap and cool water?

Having no credit score can often be just as bad as having a low one. Lenders want to know that you have a history of borrowing money and paying it back on time. After all, if you've never taken out a loan, how can a bank know that you'll pay back its money? So, having nothing on your credit report can result in low credit limits and high interest rates.

What is this passage's main idea?

No, neither of the species is "unaffected" by the relationship. Both species benefit from it.

Yes, as long as you scrub for at least twenty seconds.

The main idea is expressed in the first sentence: "Having no credit score can often be just as bad as having a low one." The other sentences in the passage tell more about this main idea.

Patients have two basic nutritional needs: they require macronutrients, the carbohydrates, fats, and proteins that provide energy; and micronutrients, which are the vitamins and elements the body needs to function properly. A good diet will provide the appropriate amount of macronutrients, or calories, to keep the patients energized and satiated without leading to weight gain while also providing necessary amounts of micronutrients. Such a diet will help patients remain comfortable and heal properly. A poor diet, on the other hand, can make recovery significantly more difficult.

What are some differences between macronutrients and micronutrients?

During the 1920s in the United States, jazz music was played by and for a more expressive and freed populace than the United States had previously seen. Women gained the right to vote and were openly seen drinking and dancing to jazz music. This period marked the emergence of the flapper, a woman determined to make a statement about her new role in society.

How was "the flapper" different from earlier generations of women in the United States?

Many patients, bedridden or otherwise, have hidden energy needs. The process of healing can be extremely energy intensive—even an immobile patient can use up vast reserves of calories as her body fights infection, knits a fracture, or heals bed sores. Patients on a low-energy diet may also develop deficiencies in micronutrients if the quality of their meals is not monitored closely.

Why might a bedridden patient fighting an infection need extra calories and/or foods that are richer in micronutrients (such as vitamins and minerals)?

Macronutrients are "the carbohydrates, fats, and proteins that provide energy," while micronutrients "are the vitamins and elements the body needs to function properly." Macronutrients provide calories (for energy); micronutrients do not.

Unlike earlier generations of U.S. women, flappers had the right to vote. They drank alcoholic beverages, danced to jazz music, and made "statement[s] about [their] new role in society."

"The process of healing can be extremely energy intensive," so a patient healing from an infection may need extra calories and extra micronutrients.

Food historians believe that popcorn is one of the earliest uses of cultivated corn. In 1948, Herbert Dick and Earle Smith discovered old popcorn dating back 4000 years in the New Mexico Bat Cave. For the Aztec Indians who called the caves home, popcorn (or *momochitl*) played an important role in society, both as a food staple and in ceremonies. The Aztecs cooked popcorn by heating sand in a fire; when it was heated, kernels were added and would pop when exposed to the heat of the sand.

What did the Aztecs do after heating sand in a fire?

Credit scores, which range from 300 to 850, are a single value that summarizes an individual's credit history. Pay your bills late? Your credit score will be lower than someone who gets that electric bill filed on the first of every month. Just paid off your massive student loans? You can expect your credit score to shoot up. The companies that compile credit scores actually keep track of all the loans, credit cards, and bill payments in your name.

What is the highest possible credit score?

Although it's a common disease, the flu is not actually highly infectious, meaning it's relatively difficult to contract. The flu can only be transmitted when individuals come into direct contact with bodily fluids of people infected with the flu or when they are exposed to expelled aerosol particles (which result from coughing and sneezing).

Which would be more likely to give you the flu: shaking hands with an infected person or sharing a drinking glass with that person? Explain why.

They added corn kernels to the heated sand; this caused the kernels to pop, forming popcorn.

The highest possible credit score is 850; the passage says that "credit scores... range from 300 to 850."

Sharing a drinking glass with an infected person would be more likely to give you the flu. Sharing a glass would probably cause you to "come into direct contact with" the infected person's saliva, a "bodily fluid." (If the person had just sneezed or coughed into her hands, shaking hands with her could give you the flu, too, but then you would have to lick your fingers to transmit the virus to your body.)

In the 1950s, scientists learned that different types of memory are handled by different parts of the brain, with the hippocampus responsible for *episodic memory*, the short-term recall of events. Researchers have since discovered that some memories are then channeled to the cortex, the outer layers of the brain that handle higher functions, where they are gradually integrated with related information to build lasting knowledge about our world.

Where is the brain's cortex located?

Being smart about taking on debt is a key factor in keeping your credit score high. If you are just starting off in the financial world, there will be multiple offers to open accounts, say, for an introductory credit card or short-term loan. But just because banks are offering you those loans doesn't make them a good idea. Instead, you should only take on debt you know you can pay back in a reasonable amount of time.

What is the author's main purpose for writing this passage?

Every morning now brought its regular duties—shops were to be visited; some new part of the town to be looked at; and the pump-room to be attended, where they paraded up and down for an hour, looking at everybody and speaking to no one. The wish of a numerous acquaintance in Bath was still uppermost with Mrs. Allen, and she repeated it after every fresh proof, which every morning brought, of her knowing nobody at all.

Where does this part of the novel take place?

The cortex is the brain's "outer layers."

To warn people not to take on debt if they cannot "pay [these debts] back in a reasonable amount of time."

In a town called Bath; Mrs. Allen is apparently on a visit to Bath and wishes to get to know new people there; however, so far she has become acquainted with "nobody at all."

While the water is heating, grind your coffee beans. Remember, the fresher the grind, the fresher the flavor of the coffee. The number of beans is entirely dependent on your personal taste. Obviously, more beans will result in a more robust flavor, while fewer beans will give your coffee a more subtle taste. The texture of the grind should be not too fine (which can lead to bitter coffee) or too large (which can lead to weak coffee).

Why do you think too-large coffee grounds can "lead to weak coffee"?

There was little leisure for speaking while [Catherine and Mr. Tilney] danced; but when they were seated at tea, she found him as agreeable as she had already given him credit for being. He talked with fluency and spirit—and there was an archness and pleasantry in his manner which interested, though it was hardly understood by her.

The excerpt says that Catherine does not understand some of what Mr. Tilney says. Why does she like speaking with him, then?

In his treatise *Politics*, Aristotle wrote, "Man is by nature a social animal; an individual who is unsocial naturally and not acciden-tally is either beneath our notice or more than human. Society is something in nature that precedes the individual. Anyone who either cannot lead the common life or is so self-sufficient as not to need to, and therefore does not partake of society, is either a beast or a god."

What are two probable reasons why Aristotle wrote this section of his treatise *Politics*?

Large (coarse) coffee grounds probably do not produce strong coffee because the hot water does not have enough access to coarse-ground coffee beans' surfaces.

"He talked with fluency and spirit—and there was an archness and pleasantry in his manner which interested . . . her." Apparently, Catherine likes Mr. Tilney's spirited, pleasant way of speaking, even though she does not understand his "archness."

One reason is to inform readers about individuals' relationship to society, and another is to express his opinions about this topic.

Human behavior cannot be understood in a vacuum; that is, our daily behaviors are inextricably linked with the social context in which they occur. Why is this important? According to social psychologist Eliot Aronson, it's important because it helps us to understand that the behaviors we witness in others may be as much a result of social influence as they are of the individual's disposition.

Why might it be important to know that someone's behavior might be caused by "social influence" rather than by that "individual's disposition"?

In general, you can take a number of basic steps to raise your credit score. First, ensure that payments are made on time. When payments are past due, it not only has a negative impact on your score, but new creditors will be reluctant to lend while you are delinquent on other accounts. Being smart about taking on debt is another key factor in keeping your credit score high.

Which phrase in the passage has the same meaning as the word *delinquent*?

If you have ever been cut off in the middle of bad city traffic, you may have immediately assumed that the offender was inconsiderate or incompetent. While this may be true, it may be equally likely that the person is dealing with an emergency situation or that they simply did not see you. According to psychologist Eliot Aronson, this tendency to attribute behaviors, especially negative behaviors, to disposition is risky and can ultimately be detrimental to us and to the other person.

What does *detrimental* mean in this passage? Explain how you know.

Answers may vary. Example: If people behave in a problematic way (for example, if they break the law), and we know their bad behavior is to some degree caused by society, we might be able to make societal changes that may change this bad behavior.

The phrase "past due" has the same meaning as *delinquent*.

It means "damaging." The author is saying that if we assume someone who cuts us off in traffic is an "inconsiderate or incompetent" person, we may be overlooking an explanation that does not support such assumptions. This could be "detrimental" to us and to the other person if, for example, we get angry and cause a car accident.

In Zimbardo's famous prison experiment, the participants, all healthy, stable, intelligent male Stanford University students, were classified as either guards or prisoners and told they would be acting their parts in a simulated prison environment.... Even giving individuals temporary power over others was enough to completely alter the way they viewed and behaved toward each other. Indeed, the behaviors Zimbardo witnessed in each of the groups were not a result of the dispositions of the participants but of the situation in which they had been placed.

What caused the participants' "behavior toward each other" to "completely alter"?

Today, social psychologists study the effect of social influence on a number of different behaviors: conformity, obedience, aggression, prejudice, and even attraction and love. The insights these researchers have gained have laid the foundation for further examination of human social behavior and, ultimately, for a refined approach to legal and social policy.

How might "social influence" affect an individual's "prejudice"?

According to Martin Seligman's 2011 book *Flourish: A Visionary New Understanding of Happiness and Well-being*, positive psychology began as an inquiry into the experiences that contribute to life satisfaction. Through his theory of authentic happiness, Seligman posited that human happiness could be understood in terms of three elements, all of which we pursue for their inherent value—positive emotions (like joy, amusement, and gratitude), engagement (the tendency to lose oneself in activity), and meaning (the extent to which one believes his or her life has purpose).

Seligman's "three elements" are engagement, meaning, and what?

The situation they were in (acting the parts of prison guards and prisoners in a "simulated prison environment") caused the participants' behavior to change.

If someone's family, friends, teachers, and other influential people hold certain prejudices, it is likely that person will grow up holding the same prejudices.

The third element is "positive emotions (like joy, amusement, and gratitude)."

In recent decades, scientific inquiry and urbanization have given birth to a new perspective on the human relationship with animal species. Studies into the common biology and ancestral origins of humans and animals, coupled with the increasing popularity of companion animals over working animals, have led scientists and laymen alike to wonder about the mental and emotional lives of other species. Concerns about animal suffering, for example, have led to major changes in a variety of industries from entertainment to food production.

Why has a "new perspective" recently developed on "the human relationship with animal[s]"?

According to veterinarian Debbie Grant, three myths are especially detrimental to the cause of animal pain management. The first of these is the myth that animals do not feel pain at all or that they feel it less intensely than humans; in fact, according to Grant, the biological mechanisms by which we experience pain are the very same mechanisms by which animals experience pain. Even the emotional reaction to a painful experience (like being afraid to return to the dentist after an unpleasant visit) is mirrored in animals.

Does this passage express facts or opinions?

It wasn't until microwave popcorn became commercially available in 1981 that at-home popcorn consumption began to grow exponentially. With the wide availability of microwaves in the United States, popcorn also began popping up in offices and hotel rooms. However, the home still remains the most popular popcorn eating spot: today, 70 percent of the 16 billion quarts of popcorn consumed annually in the United States are eaten at home.

Why did "at-home popcorn consumption [begin] to grow exponentially" in 1981?

Several factors have contributed to this new perspective; they include "scientific inquiry and urbanization" and "the increasing popularity of companion animals over working animals."

The passage expresses Dr. Debbie Grant's opinions on "myths" that "are especially detrimental to the cause of animal pain management."

Previously, most people did not have microwave ovens at home, so they had to pop corn in hot oil in a pot on a stovetop. Thus, most people who ate popcorn ate it in movie theaters or at fairs. Microwaves "became commercially available in 1981." This led to the invention of "microwave popcorn." This new product made at-home popcorn-making so much easier that more and more people began to eat popcorn at home.

Animals do not necessarily tolerate pain any better than humans do, though they may handle their pain differently. Dr. Debbie Grant emphasizes that veterinarians must be aware that a lack of obvious signs does not necessarily suggest that pain is not present: in fact, many animals, especially those that are prey animals in the wild, are likely to conceal their pain out of an instinct to hide weaknesses that may make them easy targets for predators.

Why are "prey animals in the wild . . . likely to conceal their pain"?

"Shall I tell you what you ought to say [in your journal]?" [Mr. Tilney asked].

"If you please," [replied Catherine].

"I danced with a very agreeable young man, introduced by Mr. King; had a great deal of conversation with him—seems a most extraordinary genius—hope I may know more of him. That, madam, is what I wish you to say."

"But, perhaps, I keep no journal."

"Perhaps you are not sitting in this room, and I am not sitting by you…. Not keep a journal!"

Why does Mr. Tilney call himself "a most extraordinary genius"?

In 2014, researchers of veterinary medicine at the University of Perugia in Italy completed a review of the diagnostic tools and strategies available to today's practitioners and found a number of them to be effective. Presumptive diagnosis, the first of these strategies, involves making a prediction about the animal's pain based on the observable damage to the body or body part. As with human pain, greater damage or disfigurement likely suggests more significant pain.

Where and when did veterinary researchers "[complete] a review of the diagnostic tools and strategies available to today's practitioners"?

They conceal their pain because they have "an instinct to hide weaknesses that may make them easy targets for predators."

He is trying to amuse Catherine by pretending to be conceited, but he really is not.

In 2014 at the University of Perugia in Italy.

Veterinarians can use close observation to assess changes in an animal's behavior. Unusual postures, activity levels, and movements are especially useful in determining the presence of pain, but even mood, facial expression, and appetite can be indicators. In addition to these strategies, a number of useful tools are available to help veterinarians in pain diagnosis. The most common of these is the clinical exam.

How might "unusual postures" indicate that an animal is in pain?

[*The following passage is adapted from an article entitled "The Solar System and Beyond Is Awash with Water," published online by the National Aeronautics and Space Administration in April 2015.*]

As NASA missions explore our solar system and search for new worlds, they are finding water in surprising places. Water is but one piece of our search for habitable planets and life beyond Earth, yet it links many seemingly unrelated worlds in surprising ways.

"NASA science activities have provided a wave of amazing findings related to water in recent years that inspire us to continue investigating our origins and the fascinating possibilities for other worlds, and life, in the universe," said Ellen Stofan, chief scientist for the agency.

Who is Ellen Stofan (what is her job)?

The chemical elements in water, hydrogen and oxygen, are some of the most abundant elements in the universe. Astronomers see the signature of water in giant molecular clouds between the stars, in disks of material that represent newborn planetary systems, and in the atmospheres of giant planets orbiting other stars. There are several worlds thought to possess liquid water beneath their surfaces, and many more that have water in the form of ice or vapor.

Why might astronomers be interested in finding water on planets other than Earth?

For example, if a dog has hip pain, she may stand, sit, or lie down in different ways than she used to do. Someone who has been observing the dog for a long time will be able to see such differences. Also, a vet may be able to tell that such postures are not typical of dogs without hip pain.

She is (or was in 2015) chief scientist at NASA, the National Aeronautics and Space Administration.

Because planets with water might also be inhabited with living creatures.

Water is found in primitive bodies like comets and asteroids, and dwarf planets like Ceres. The atmospheres and interiors of the four giant planets—Jupiter, Saturn, Uranus and Neptune—are thought to contain enormous quantities of the wet stuff, and their moons and rings have substantial water ice.

Perhaps the most surprising water worlds are the five icy moons of Jupiter and Saturn that show strong evidence of oceans beneath their surfaces: Ganymede, Europa and Callisto at Jupiter, and Enceladus and Titan at Saturn.

How many of Saturn's moons are "icy"?

...forming his features into a set smile, and affectedly softening his voice, [Mr. Tilney] added, with a simpering air, "Have you been long in Bath, madam?"

"About a week, sir," replied Catherine, trying not to laugh.

"Really!" with affected astonishment.

"Why should you be surprised, sir?"

"Why, indeed!" said he, in his natural tone. "But some emotion must appear to be raised by your reply, and surprise is more easily assumed, and not less reasonable than any other. Now let us go on. Were you never here before, madam?"

Why is Mr. Tilney "simpering" and acting "affectedly"?

The Scream of Nature by Edvard Munch has four different versions: two paintings and two pastels. The Munch Museum in Oslo holds a painted version and a pastel version, while the National Gallery in Oslo holds the other painting. In 1994 the National Gallery's version was stolen, and in 2004 the painting at the Munch Museum was stolen at gunpoint in the middle of the day. Both paintings were eventually recovered. In 2012, the second pastel version was sold at auction for almost $120 million.

How many versions of the artwork were stolen, and how many versions were sold?

Two: Enceladus and Titan.

He is probably trying to amuse Catherine by making fun of the silly way society people make conversation. They ask boring, predictable questions and pretend to be "astonished" by boring, predictable answers.

Two versions, both paintings, were stolen and have been recovered. One version, a pastel, sold at auction in 2012 for almost $120 million.

Understanding the distribution of water in our solar system tells us a great deal about how the planets, moons, comets and other bodies formed 4.5 billion years ago from the disk of gas and dust that surrounded our sun. The space closer to the sun was hotter and drier than the space farther from the sun, which was cold enough for water to condense.

Do the planets closest to our sun have water on them? Explain why you think so.

Keep an eye on unpaid student loans, medical bills, and parking tickets, all of which can take a negative toll on your credit score. In fact, your credit score will take a major hit from any bill that's sent to a collection agency, so it's in your best interest to avoid letting bills get to that point. Many organizations will agree to keep bills away from collection agencies if you set up a fee payment system.

What does a collection agency do?

Veterinarians have a unique challenge when it comes to diagnosing their patients. Unlike doctors, who typically have the benefit of discussing their patients' concerns, veterinarians cannot ask their patients whether and where they are experiencing discomfort. Additionally, veterinarians must be aware of the survival instinct of many animals to mask pain in response to stressful experiences or foreign environments. For these reasons, diagnostic tools and strategies are instrumental in the effective practice of veterinary medicine.

Why is it easier for doctors to diagnose painful illnesses and injuries than it is for veterinarians?

The planets closest to our sun probably do not have water because it is too hot and dry there. The passage says that "the space farther from the sun . . . was cold enough for water to condense."

It tries to collect overdue bills from people who owe money; it works for companies that lend people money.

Doctors' patients are humans, who can tell their doctors "whether and where they are experiencing discomfort." Obviously, animals cannot use language to communicate with vets.

The amount of water in the giant planet Jupiter holds a critical missing piece to the puzzle of our solar system's formation. Jupiter was likely the first planet to form, and it contains most of the material that wasn't incorporated into the sun. The leading theories about its formation rest on the amount of water the planet soaked up.

Do scientists think Jupiter "soaked up" a great deal of water, only a little, or none? What makes you think so?

In 1989, almost a million Chinese university students descended on central Beijing, protesting for increased democracy. The world was stunned when, on July 4, Chinese troops and security police stormed the square, firing into the crowd. Chaos erupted with some students trying to fight back by throwing stones and setting fire to military vehicles. Tens of thousands more attempted to flee. While official numbers were never given, observers estimated anywhere from 300 to thousands of people were killed, while 10,000 were arrested.

It can be inferred from the passage that Chinese authorities killed and arrested student protesters for what reason?

After World War I, some American writers, raised on the values of the prewar world, felt frustrated with what they viewed as the superficiality and materialism of postwar American culture. Many of them, like Ernest Hemingway and F. Scott Fitzgerald, fled to Paris, where they became known as the "lost generation," creating a trove of literary works criticizing their home culture and delving into their own feelings of alienation.

Use context to define the word *trove* in this passage.

They probably think Jupiter "soaked up" a great deal of water. The passage says that Jupiter is a "giant planet," and that it was "likely the first planet to form, and it contains most of the material that wasn't incorporated into the sun." This implies that it "soaked up" a lot of the water that first existed in our solar system.

They probably killed and arrested the protesters to assert their authority and to quash demands for increased democracy; clearly, the existing Chinese government leaders did not want a more democratic government.

A treasure trove is a collection of valuable metals, coins, and jewels, so a "trove of literary works" must be a collection of valuable literary works: a trove must be a collection of valuable items.

Once your coffee beans are ground and the water has reached the perfect temperature, you're ready to brew. A French press (which we recommend), allows you to control brewing time and provide a thorough brew. Pour the grounds into the press, then pour the hot water over the grounds and let it steep. The brew shouldn't require more than 5 minutes, although those of you who like your coffee a bit harsher can leave it longer. Finally, use the plunger to remove the grounds and pour.

What should you do after "pour[ing] the grounds into the press"?

During the 1920s in the United States, jazz music provided the soundtrack for the explosion of African American art and culture now known as the Harlem Renaissance. In addition to Ella Fitzgerald and Louis Armstrong, numerous musicians, including Duke Ellington, Fats Waller, and Bessie Smith, promoted their distinctive and complex music as an integral part of the emerging African American culture.

How did jazz music affect the Harlem Renaissance?

There are many situations when measuring temperature orally isn't an option. Some people, like agitated patients or fussy babies, won't be able to sit still long enough for an accurate reading. In these situations, it's best to use a thermometer that works much more quickly, such as one that measures temperature in the ear or at the temporal artery.

In what situation is it "best to use a thermometer that works much more quickly, such as one that measures temperature in the ear or at the temporal artery"?

After "pour[ing] the grounds into the press," you should "pour the hot water over the grounds and let it steep."

Jazz music formed an important part of the Harlem Renaissance and "provided the soundtrack" for this cultural "explosion." During this time, most jazz musicians were African American; the Harlem Renaissance was an African American cultural movement centered in Harlem, a neighborhood in New York City.

When a patient cannot "sit still long enough for an accurate reading"; two examples of such a patient are an agitated person or a fussy baby.

It had been a long morning for Julia. She'd been woken up early by the sound of lawn mowers outside her window, and despite her best efforts, had been unable to get back to sleep. So, she'd reluctantly got out of bed, showered, and prepared her morning cup of coffee. At least, she tried to anyway. In the kitchen, she'd discovered she was out of regular coffee and had to settle for a decaffeinated cup instead.

Which sentence expresses this paragraph's main idea?

Social psychologists have been studying the effect of societal influences on human behavior for decades, and a number of fascinating findings have been the result. Together, these discoveries have shed light on one clear truth—that human behavior cannot be understood in a vacuum; that is, our daily behaviors are inextricably linked with the social context in which they occur.

What evidence does the author give to support the argument that "human behavior cannot be understood in a vacuum"?

Recently, the courts have grappled with questions about the hiring company's responsibility in maintaining fair labor practices. Companies argue that they delegate that authority to the subcontractors, while unions and other worker advocate groups argue that companies still have a legal obligation to the workers who contribute to their business.

Why might companies prefer using subcontracting services to hiring full-time employees?

The first sentence: "It had been a long morning for Julia." All the other sentences explain what makes the morning "long" (and annoying) for Julia.

The author says that social psychologists have made "fascinating findings" that "shed light on" the premise that "our daily behaviors are inextricably linked with the social context in which they occur."

It is probably cheaper to use subcontracting services. For full-time employees, businesses must pay for benefits such as sick days and health care.

It's easy to forget that the story of Earth's water, from gentle rains to raging rivers, is intimately connected to the larger story of our solar system and beyond. But our water came from somewhere— every world in our solar system got its water from the same shared source. So it's worth considering that the next glass of water you drink could easily have been part of a comet, or an ocean moon, or a long-vanished sea on the surface of Mars.

How does the author seem to feel about the information in this passage?

"I see what you think of me," said [Mr. Tilney] gravely—"I shall make but a poor figure in your journal tomorrow."

"My journal!" [replied Catherine].

"Yes, I know exactly what you will say: Friday, went to the Lower Rooms; wore my sprigged muslin robe with blue trimmings—plain black shoes—appeared to much advantage; but was strangely harassed by a queer, half-witted man, who would make me dance with him, and distressed me by his nonsense."

"Indeed I shall say no such thing."

Is Mr. Tilney really "harassing" or "distress[ing]" Catherine? Explain.

The author seems awed by the fact that Earth's water—in fact, our drinking water—probably came from "part of a comet, or an ocean moon, or a long-vanished sea on the surface of Mars."

No, he is probably trying to amuse Catherine by making fun of the content and style of young women's journals and by calling himself "a queer, half-witted man."

What is a subject?

What is a predicate?

CPSIA information can be obtained
at www.ICGtesting.com
Printed in the USA
LVHW051042030121
675543LV00030B/797